QUICK and EASY PATCHWORK on the SEWING MACHINE

Step-by-Step Instructions and Full-Size Templates for 12 Quilt Blocks

SUSAN AYLSWORTH
MURWIN

AND

SUZZY CHALFANT
PAYNE

DOVER PUBLICATIONS, INC.
NEW YORK

Published in Canada by General Publishing Company, Ltd., 30 Lesmill Road, Don Mills, Toronto, Ontario.
Published in the United Kingdom by Constable and Company, Ltd., 10 Orange Street, London WC2H 7EG.

Quick and Easy Patchwork on the Sewing Machine; Step-by-Step Instructions and Full-Size Templates for 12 Quilt Blocks is a new work, first published by Dover Publications, Inc., in 1979.

International Standard Book Number: 0-486-23770-2
Library of Congress Catalog Card Number: 78-74751

Manufactured in the United States of America
Dover Publications, Inc.
180 Varick Street
New York, N.Y. 10014

To our students: who said it first; "you ought to write a book!"

To our children: who survived constant quilt clutter, more than occasional soup and sandwich suppers, and mommies who were always on the telephone.

To our husbands: who survived those long distance telephone bills, and arranged their own jobs to enable us to cross the 300 mile distance between our homes—frequently enough to get this done.

To each other: because we were able to share our different aptitudes, gently pushing each other towards growth and change, until this system of quilt making was developed.

CONTENTS

INTRODUCTION

We began as next-door neighbors. We became friends. Years passed, and each of us moved several times. Our children arrived. In between these events in our lives, like many young women in the sixties, both of us were experimenting with various handicrafts—knitting, crewel, needlepoint, dressmaking, rug hooking, and so forth. Although our homes have been 300 miles apart in recent years, and it has been impossible for us to pursue any hobby together regularly, somehow, independently, we arrived at an identical first choice of a craft, patchwork and quilting.

We came to this pursuit from different directions, however. The working style of one of us was to get a job done, neatly and attractively, but quickly, above all. Her goal was to have a completed product that could be used now. She naturally chose the sewing machine for making her patchwork. The other preferred perfection to speed. A project would be finished, and could be used, only when it was finished right. She chose to make her patchwork by hand.

We soon knew we were dissatisfied with both of our sewing methods. Although the machine sewer could precisely piece in only a few hours "Around the World" and "Irish Chain" quilts, which use the square, the simplest geometric shape, she had to accept a slower progress with the more complicated geometric forms, such as triangles, hexagons and diamonds. At times perfect accuracy had to be sacrificed with these shapes. The sewing machine would jog along on its own course, heedless of her desire for exactly matching seam joints. The hand sewer, on the other hand, could tackle almost any pattern, with any combination of geometric shapes. Hand piecing is easy. One seam allowance is seldom stitched across another, so the allowances are free and can be manipulated for small errors; even the most complex star pattern will always lie flat. But the hand-piecing process is laboriously slow, and this handsewer became discouraged with her limited production.

For a time we merely shared our different frustrations with our craft, in letters or during occasional visits. We seemed stuck, until one family weekend together we realized we might combine our knowledge about patterns, geometric forms, techniques, the art of patchwork, and the sewing machine. Perhaps we could discover simple, direct, fast methods for machine piecing the beautiful traditional patterns that we really wanted to do.

We had already explored the available quilting books and knew they could not help us. The traditional patterns were often inaccurately drawn or shown in odd sizes, making it impossible to complete a quilt without major modifications. Some books provided patterns without instructions. Others gave general directions to be adapted by the reader for specific patterns. Occasionally, a book would make a suggestion for machine piecing; but we never found a book with detailed instructions for piecing any pattern on the sewing machine.

We made a list of our favorite patterns—and a plan. In our separate homes, we would attack every pattern, doing each one over and over on scrap materials, always searching for secrets and shortcuts. Would it ever be possible to sew "Storm at Sea," "Three-Dimensional Dahlia," or "Drunkard's Path" quickly and accurately with perfect points, angles, or curves?

The "Eight-Pointed Star" was our first success. In our independent practice trials each of us found different tricks. Then we combined it all. If the "Eight-Pointed Star" could work, we knew any pattern could. And on we went through our list of patterns.

Best of all, we had discovered we could be a team, able to share, and learn, and work together. Finding new skills for the sewing machine was easier for the machine sewer, and she devised the majority of them. Her shortcuts, such as chain sewing and layered cutting, were merely logical, she felt. Attempting every handsewing technique on the sewing machine (before discarding some of them forever), and testing the machine sewer's maneuvers became the main tasks for the handsewer.

We could not hide the information we were accumulating. It was a natural development that we became patchwork and quilting teachers. Working and studying together long distance, and with much growth and change for each of us, we finally designed our course: "Patchwork on the Sewing Machine—Create a Quilt in 7 Weeks." Our students repeatedly proved the speed and success of these patchwork methods with the high-quality quilts they created in every seven-week series. Now we are pleased that through the medium of this book, we are able to share our ideas with many more quiltmakers.

HOW TO
USE THIS BOOK

This book contains twelve well-loved patchwork patterns, which have been used by many generations of American quilters. We present them now in a practical, convenient format for modern quilters. The patterns are precision designed to a finished size of 14'' square so that they can be used collectively to make a sampler quilt such as the one on the front cover. All of the pattern pieces are given in actual-size templates printed on heavyweight paper in the template section of this book. Because our methods are intended for sewing machine piecing, the templates include the 1/4'' seam allowance.

On pages 5–9, we present our *Techniques for Machine Piecing.* Read these pages first. Become familiar with the new terms. Even practice a few of the techniques. These pages are intended to be your handy reference guide to time-saving ideas. Use them as such. We've saved visual confusion on the pattern pages by not repeating these hints every time they occur in individual blocks; instead, we have referred you back to the various hints in the *Techniques for Machine Piecing* Section, pages 5–9.

When you have selected your pattern, read the instructions given with that pattern. Some patterns require more detailed instructions than others. Trust us. We want to eliminate hocus-pocus, mystique, and unnecessary tasks from the art of quiltmaking; therefore, we give extra details only when we believe that they are absolutely necessary. Follow the directions carefully, and we think you will have excellent results.

The patterns are arranged, in general, from the most basic of the collection, "Road to California," to the most complex, "Three-Dimensional Dahlia." This order progresses through the geometric shapes: square, rectangle, triangle, diamond, parallelogram, hexagon, curve and the combinations of two or more of these shapes. These twelve quilt blocks cover most of the common problems found in patchwork. If you are doing a sampler quilt, we recommend that you follow the order of the patterns as given in the book.

For many quilt blocks we suggest light, medium, dark or bright shadings for fabrics, rather than specific colors. Substitute your own color selections for our shading suggestions as you plan and sew the patterns. You can, of course, reverse our suggestions as long as you maintain sharp contrast where indicated.

Fabrics that are 100% cotton are the most satisfactory. Polyester-cotton blends will work if they feel like cotton. Fabrics with a silky feeling or with a loose weave will not feed smoothly under the pressure foot of the sewing machine. This will cause seam edges to slip, and then your angles, joints and curves will not match accurately.

Because we are women of the twentieth century, we are presenting as many modern methods and shortcuts as we can. We hope that your actual sewing will be quick, simple and accurate so that you will enjoy the process of quiltmaking as much as the finished product.

TECHNIQUES FOR MACHINE PIECING

1. SEAM ALLOWANCE

Use 1/4'' seam allowances on all seams. Use whatever method is most convenient for you, but it is essential to have a dependable method of following the 1/4'' seam allowance on your sewing machine.

In general, seam allowances should be pressed to one side and not opened.

2. TEMPLATES

All of the pattern pieces are given in actual-size templates printed on heavyweight paper in the template section of this book. Locate the designated template and cut around the templates freehand. With rubber cement, glue the template onto heavy cardboard, such as a medium weight illustration board. Then cut precisely on the template cutting lines. Use sandpaper to smooth any rough edges.

3. LAYERED CUTTING

Straighten the grain of the fabric. Fold the fabric lengthwise, wrong sides together as it comes off the bolt. Turn the fold edge to meet the selvage edges, making four layers. On the crosswise grain, measure and cut a strip of cloth large enough to accommodate a given template, with 1/4'' to spare on either side. For example, for a 2 1/2'' square, cut a 3'' by 11'' strip as shown in the diagram. Fold this strip as many times as the template will allow (from four to sixteen layers). Grain lines are indicated on each template. Lay the template on the fabric grain. Hold the template firmly and trim around it, using heavyweight, extra sharp scissors. Sandpaper glued on the back will prevent large templates from slipping.

Extra hints for cutting specific geometric shapes:

A. Triangles: Cut the two right angle edges first and the long side last.

B. Curves: Cut the straight edges first and the curve last.

C. Diamonds: Carefully observe the grain lines on the templates to ensure two bias sides and two straight sides for diamond patches.

D. Parallelograms: This is an asymmetrical figure having a right side and a left side. This is not a problem for the layered method of cutting because half of the layers of material within each folded strip are right side up and half are wrong side up.

E. Trapezoids: The particular trapezoid template used in the "See Saw" pattern must be laid right side up on the right side of the fabric, for every patch that is cut.

4. STRIP CUTTING

Prepare and fold the fabric lengthwise into quarters, as in layered cutting above. Lay the strip template on the fabric, parallel to the straightened edge of the cross-grain, but 1/2'' or so above it. For the first strip, mark on both lengthwise sides of the template, using a fineline felt-tip pen. Succeeding strips can be laid against the previous mark, so only the upper side of the template needs to be traced. Keep fabric flat and carefully cut along your marking lines, as you would cut a dress pattern. When unfolded, the strips will measure 1 1/2'' by 44'' or 1 1/2'' by 36'', depending on width of fabric used. Strip cutting is used for the strip templates in "Rail Fence" and "Log Cabin."

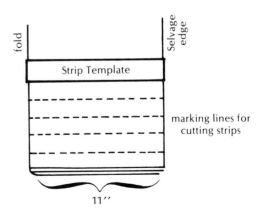

5. ACCURATE PIECING

Accurate piecing is easier when corners and edges of pieces are matched perfectly before seaming. For example, the right angle edges of a triangle matched exactly to the right angle edges of a square.

6. CHAIN SEWING SMALL UNITS

When combining the pieces of all the small units required to complete a block (such as sewing the two small triangles into squares in "Road to California") simply fit these pieces right sides together and feed all the needed units through the machine, assembly-line fashion, without clipping any threads, so that an approximate 1" chain connects each unit. Cut the chain to separate the units, and proceed with the pattern instructions.

7. CHAIN SEWING THE ENTIRE BLOCK

When assembling a block of squares (such as the assembled squares in "Drunkard's Path" or "Road to California") lay out all the pieces to form the pattern, following the diagram of the pattern. Sew all the rows vertically, "chain" fashion, as described above in #6 "Chain Sewing Small Units".

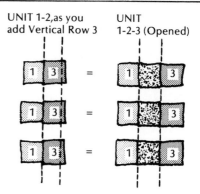

The chain in fabric as you add vertical Row 3.

There are two acceptable ways to do this:

A. With a visible chain of about 1" connecting each unit, as in the above diagrams. This allows you to fold back the top edges when seaming the long horizontal rows, in order to "butt" the seam joints and then pin the seam allowances on each side of the joint (as described in 8A "Butting Seams") for perfectly matched seams.

B. With no visible chain at all connecting each unit, as in the diagram below. Stop the machine a few stitches before finishing the short seam joining Row A-1 to Row A-2 (Unit 1-2). Fit pieces B-1 and B-2 right sides together, and slide them under the pressure foot so that they exactly touch the unit just sewn. Continue with the other rows.

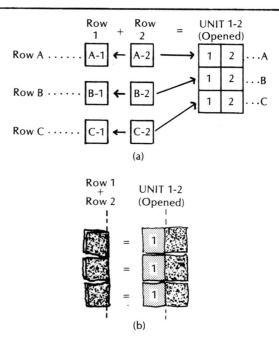

(a) Chain sewing the entire block with no visible chain connecting units. (b) How the invisible chain looks in fabric as you add vertical row 3. Note that the vertically connected rows of Units 1-2 will dangle strangely because they are not yet joined by the horizontal seams.

(a) Vertical row 1 joined to vertical row 2 making a chain of vertical units 1-2. (b) Vertical row 3 added to all units 1-2. Continue adding vertical rows until the block is completed.

This allows you to eliminate pins entirely when sewing the long horizontal rows of Row A to Row B, etc., but you *must* finger press the seam allowance of each seam joint to the opposite direction, as described below in 8A "Butting Seams".

8. MATCHING HORIZONTAL SEAM JOINTS

A. Butting Seams: When preparing to sew horizontal rows together in a long seam, fit the rows right sides together and fold back the top edges of the seam allowance, so you can see the vertical seam joints on the inside. *Butt* these joints against each other perfectly. Finger press or pin the vertical seam allowance on the joint of one row in one direction, and the seam allowance of the matching joint of the other row in the opposite direction.

A correctly "butted" seam joint will feel flat, without ridges or bumps.

If pins are used, pin through each seam allowance, not through the seam joint itself. Do this across the row as often as necessary.

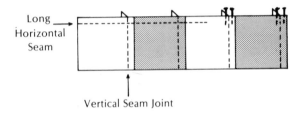

For perfectly matched joints, it is more important to have the seam allowances go in opposite directions than to have seam allowances go towards the darker fabric.

B. Stitching through the Λ's: When triangles or diamonds meet in four to eight points in a long horizontal seam, have the seam lines of one full triangle or diamond face up, so you can stitch through the exact inverted "V". (Λ)

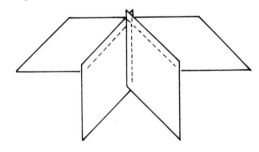

C. Hold Pin Technique: When triangles or diamonds meet in four to eight points in a long horizontal seam, align the exact centers of the two halves right sides together and "butt seams" as described. Insert a "Hold Pin" through the (Λ) of the visible triangle or diamond, being sure it emerges precisely through the (Λ) of the visible triangle or

diamond on the back, and that it holds the two halves level.

Finger press the center seam allowances in opposite directions and pin both. Remove the "Hold Pin". Stitch the seam.

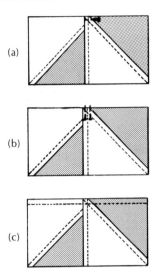

(a) Right sides together, "butt" the seams and insert "Hold Pin" through the Λ. (b) Pin seam allowances in opposite directions. (c) A correctly sewn long horizontal seam.

The "Hold Pin Technique" is used in "Variable Stars," "Summer Stars," "See Saw," "Eight Pointed Star" and "Storm at Sea".

D. Pinning Tails: When sewing pieces with long tails, such as the diamonds (a) in the "Eight-Pointed Star," or the triangles (b) in "Variable Stars," place a pin once about 1/2" from the tip of the tail. This prevents slippage of the pieces when sewing, making these narrow angles more accurate; thus, a more perfect match of four to eight points in any long seam will be possible.

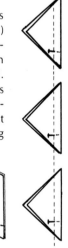

9. SETTING IN

"Setting in" is necessary whenever angled pieces are being inserted and the design of the block prohibits sewing across seam allowances. The seam allowances at the corner of any "set in" seam are free and will fan in any direction.

A. Back Stitch Method: Drop the sewing machine needle into the pieces that are being seamed, exactly 1/4" from both raw edges. Lock this seam by sewing forward two stitches, then back-stitching two stitches. Sew forward to the end of the seam.

B. Fine Stitch Method: The beginning of the "set in" seam can also be locked by changing the stitch length to "fine," sewing a few stitches, then returning the stitch to its customary size for the remainder of the seam.

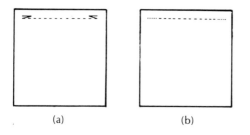

(a) Back stitch method. (b) Fine stitch method.

Seams that end with "setting in" also must be locked by one of the above methods.

The term "set in" is used in: "Grandmother's Flower Garden," "Eight-Pointed Star," and "Dresden Plate".

10. SEWING CURVES

When sewing curves, always have the patch with the clipped, concave curve on top, because you are easing this to fit the smaller convex patch (which is on the bottom). Match the right angle corners of the two patches and pin as shown.

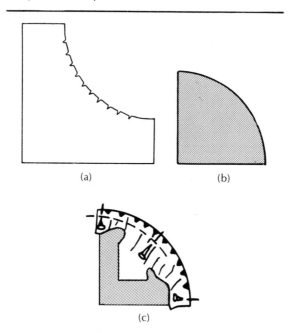

(a) "Crescent Square" patch with clipped, concave curve. (b) "Wedge" patch with convex curve. (c) "Crescent Square" eased and pinned on top of "Wedge".

11. BORDER-AS-YOU-GO

Following the instructions given in #4 "Strip Cutting," cut two 1 1/2" by 44" strips. Apply to the sides of block being bordered, following the diagram below,

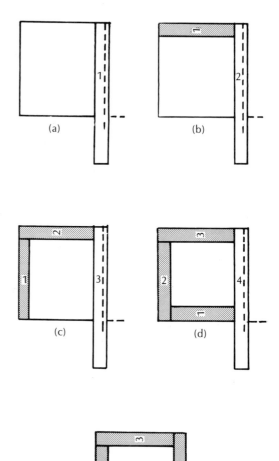

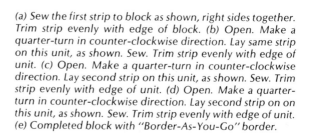

(a) Sew the first strip to block as shown, right sides together. Trim strip evenly with edge of block. (b) Open. Make a quarter-turn in counter-clockwise direction. Lay same strip on this unit, as shown. Sew. Trim strip evenly with edge of unit. (c) Open. Make a quarter-turn in counter-clockwise direction. Lay second strip on this unit, as shown. Sew. Trim strip evenly with edge of unit. (d) Open. Make a quarter-turn in counter-clockwise direction. Lay second strip on on this unit, as shown. Sew. Trim strip evenly with edge of unit. (e) Completed block with "Border-As-You-Go" border.

"Border-As-You-Go" is used in the "Rail Fence" block.

12. APPLIQUÉ TECHNIQUES

A. Pressing Angled Edges: Outside angled edges, which are 90 degrees (like "Dresden Plate") or obtuse (like "Grandmother's Flower Garden") will overlap each other neatly, without bulk, when you press under the 1/4" seam allowance with a hot steam iron. This is the only preparation needed before appliquéing such edges.

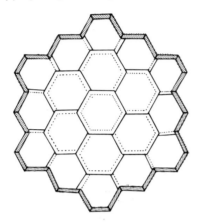

B. Pressing Curved Edges: The easiest way to prepare a curve for appliqué is to use a pressing template, which is slightly smaller than the finished size of the patchwork piece. The cardboard used on the template pages in this book is the correct thickness for a pressing template.

First, press the back of the block to be appliquéd, so that seam allowances go towards dark fabrics, whenever possible. Next, insert the pressing template under the seam allowances. Finally, with a hot steam iron, press the 1/4" seam allowance of the curved edge of the patch over the curved edge of the pressing template.

100% cotton fabrics will hold a sharper crease than polyester-blend fabrics.

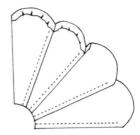

C. Invisible Appliqué Stitch: The invisible appliqué stitch is a running stitch on the back of the backing fabric, and a running stitch in the crease of the fold of the piece being appliquéd. When done correctly, both stitches are invisible on the front.

Use a single thread with a knot. Bring the needle and thread through the backing fabric, from back to front. Take a small stitch in the crease of the fold of the top piece. Then, insert the point of the needle into the backing, exactly behind the spot where the thread emerged in the fold, and *below* the level of the top fold. Take another running stitch in the back; then a running stitch in the fold on the top; and so forth. Every three or four stitches, gently tug the thread, and all the stitches will disappear.

1. Never angle your stitch, or the thread will show like a hemming stitch.
2. Never have fabrics of both backing and top on the needle at the same time, or your stitches will show like a hemming stitch.
3. Use commercial quilting thread which is stronger than polyester-cotton thread and is coated to prevent knotting.

THE QUILTS

ROAD TO CALIFORNIA

The two templates used to make this block appear on Plate 1.

1. Layer cut the following pieces. See *Layered Cutting* (3).

Template A .... 25 medium fabric
Template B .... 24 light fabric
Template B .... 24 dark fabric

2. Chain sew light and dark triangles, made from Template B, into squares. See *Chain Sewing Small Units* (6) and *Pinning Tails* (8D).

3. Open and press the seam allowance towards the dark triangle. Clip the tails.

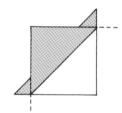

4. Following the block diagram, lay out the squares made from Template A and the assembled squares made from Template B to form the pattern.

5. Sew the entire block. See *Chain Sewing the Entire Block* (7A) and *Butting Seams* (8A).

We feel this is one of the few blocks that should have a color recommendation. If your goals are a distinctly visible "road," and the impression of two "Variable Stars" on that "road," choose a medium tone fabric for the squares and a definite light and dark contrast for the triangles.

RAIL FENCE

The two templates used to make this block appear on Plates 2 and 3.

1. Choose four 44″ wide fabrics, two dominant in color or print.
2. Use Template A to cut one strip of each fabric. The actual measurement of each strip will be 1 1/2″ × 44″. See *Strip Cutting* (4).
3. Seam four strips together, starting and ending with a dominant fabric.
4. Press. The four strips sewed together will measure 4 1/2″ wide.

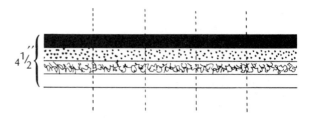

5. Using Template B, cut this pieced fabric into nine squares.
6. Arrange the squares following the block diagram.
7. Chain sew the entire block. See *Chain Sewing the Entire Block* (7A) and *Butting Seams* (8A).
8. Add the border, using Template A. See *Border-As-You-Go* (11).

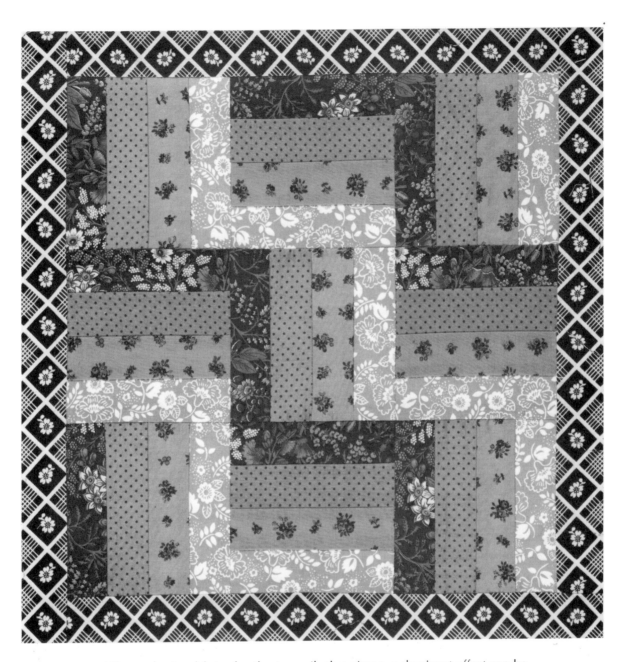

When selecting fabrics for the two rails that zigzag, a dominant effect can be achieved in several ways:

1. Choose white, or any solid color
2. Choose a print with bright colors or a strong design
3. Choose three fabrics or prints in tones of one color with the fourth fabric in a completely different color.

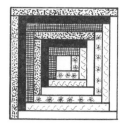

LOG CABIN

The two templates used to make this block appear on Plate 4.

1. Choose three light 44″ wide fabrics and three dark 44″ wide fabrics for the strips. (In addition, you will need a bright fabric for the small square in the center of the block.)

2. Use Template A to cut one strip from each of the light and dark fabrics. (The actual measurement of each strip will be 1 1/2″ × 44″.) See *Strip Cutting* (4).

3. Using Template B, cut one square from the bright fabric.

4. Beginning with a light strip, sew the strip to the square, as shown, right sides together. Trim strip evenly with the edge of the square.

5. Open. Make a quarter turn in a counter-clockwise direction. Lay the same strip on this unit, as shown. Sew. Trim the strip evenly with the edge of the unit.

6. Continue making quarter turns of the unit and adding strips in a counter-clockwise direction. Finger press all seam allowances away from the center square as you sew.

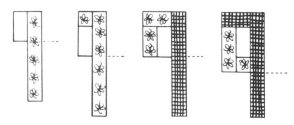

7. Alternate light and dark strips, using the same strip twice before selecting a new strip. To create the block, follow the numbered order in the diagram:

> #1 and #2 = light strip 1
> #3 and #4 = dark strip 1
> #5 and #6 = light strip 2
> #7 and #8 = dark strip 2
> #9 and #10 = light strip 3
> #11 and #12 = dark strip 3.

Repeat the above order and colors for strips 13–24.

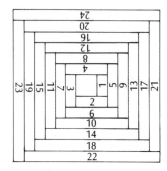

"Courthouse Steps," a variation of the "Log Cabin" block, can be created by a slightly different arrangement of the strips, as shown below.

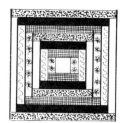

Of all patchwork patterns, "Log Cabin" is now the quickest and most economical to make. It is one of the oldest quilt designs and has always been popular. This assembly method of "Cut and Measure As-You-Go" should assure its continued popularity with contemporary quilters.

VARIABLE STARS

The two templates used to make this block and its variations appear on Plate 5.

1. Layer cut the following pieces. See *Layered Cutting* (3).

  Template A . . . . .8 dark fabric
  Template A . . . . .4 medium fabric I
  Template A . . . . . . .4 medium fabric II
  Template A . . . . .16 light fabric

2. Chain sew light and dark triangles into squares and light and medium triangles into squares. See *Chain Sewing Small Units* (6) and *Pinning Tails* (8D).

3. Open and press the seam allowance towards the dark triangle. Clip the tails.

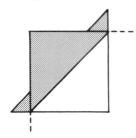

4. Following the block diagram, arrange the assembled squares to form the pattern.

5. Sew the entire block. See *Chain Sewing the Entire Block* (7A) and *Matching Horizontal Seam Joints* (8).

Some "Variable Stars" use a combination of a triangle and a square, and in order to make these variations it will be necessary to make the square from Template B on Plate 5.

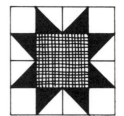

Variation One

Variation Two

Variation Three

"Variable Stars" are among the earliest pieced quilt designs and demonstrate the American pioneer woman's determination to cut and manipulate her scraps into beautiful geometric patterns.

"Variable Stars" are like ordered picture puzzles. You can compose your own, by exploiting the arrangement possibilities of squares and triangles, shades and colors, as you see them.

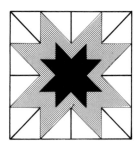

SUMMER STARS

The three templates used to make this block appear on Plate 6.

1. Layer cut the following pieces. See *Layered Cutting* (3) and *Parallelograms* (3D).

> Template A .....8 dark or bright fabric
> Template A ....8 medium fabric
> Template B ....8 medium fabric

2. Layer cut the following pieces. See *Layered Cutting* (3) and *Triangles* (3A).

> Template C............16 light fabric

3. Assemble one quarter of the block at a time.
Side One:
(a) Position a dark parallelogram made from Template A over a medium parallelogram made from Template A so that they are off center by the 1/4″ seam allowance.

(b) Seam. Open and press the seam allowance toward the dark fabric.

(c) Position a parallelogram made from Template B over the "A/A" unit so that they are off center by the 1/4″ seam allowance.

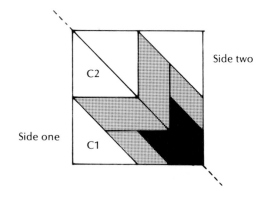

(d) Seam. Open.
(e) Add the triangles made from Template C in numbered order according to the diagram. See *Accurate Piecing* (5).
Side Two:
(a) Position a medium parallelogram made from Template A over a dark parallelogram made from Template A so that they are off center by the 1/4″ seam allowance.
(b) Seam, and continue as for side one.

Join Side One and Side Two in a long, diagonal seam, completing one quarter of the block.
4. Assemble the entire block following the block diagram and matching the joints perfectly for a clearly defined star.
5. Sew the center seam. See *Matching Horizontal Seam Joints* (8A, 8B and 8C).

The advantage of the "Summer Star" is the straight seam construction without "setting in". The "star within a star" or sunburst effect is achieved by strong contrast in fabric selection. This block is equally dramatic when fabrics are arranged in reverse order from our sample, with a light center star framed by a medium outer star and a dark outside edge.

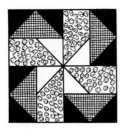

SEE SAW

The three templates used to make this block appear on Plate 7.

1. Layer cut the following pieces. See *Layered Cutting* (3).

Template A . . . . .4 light fabric
Template A . . . . .8 dark fabric
Template B . . . . 4 bright fabric

2. Cut the following pieces. See *Trapezoids* (3E).

Template C . . . . .4 dominant print

3. This pattern is made by constructing two basic units and then combining them to make the finished block.

Unit One:

(a) Sew dark triangle made from Template A to triangle made from Template B. See *Accurate Piecing (5)*.

(b) Open. Clip tails.

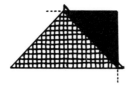

(c) Sew a second dark triangle made from Template A to the unit; open and clip tails.
(d) Repeat the above instructions, making three additional units.

Unit Two:

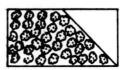

(a) Sew a light triangle made from Template A to trapezoid made from Template C as shown.

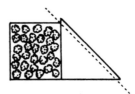

(b) Open. Clip tails.
(c) Repeat the above instructions, making three additional units.
4. Following the block diagram, make four squares combining Unit One and Unit Two.
5. Assemble the four squares to complete the block. See *Matching Horizontal Seam Joints* (8A, 8B and 8C).

"See Saw" is an easy block to construct; the only joint to match is the eight-pointed center.

Our suggestions for fabric prints and color shadings will create one type of graphic effect in this simple block. A very light or white pinwheel will seem to whirl with the large bright triangles, which will then appear to turn counter-clockwise. The trapezoids meeting in the center of the block are the fulcrum for the apparent movement. Choosing a dominant or busy print, rather than a solid color fabric, for these extra-large patches, will keep them from overwhelming the balance of the pattern. "See Saw," colored as shown, with dark corners, also makes an attractive pillow.

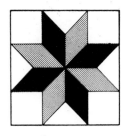

EIGHT-POINTED STAR

The three templates used to make this block appear on Plates 8 and 9.

1. Layer cut the following pieces. See *Layered Cutting* (3).

    Template A......8 print fabric
                      (Use 2 to 4 contrasting prints.)
    Template B......4 light fabric
    Template C......4 light fabric

2. Assemble the top and bottom halves of the star according to the following instructions and diagrams.

Top Half:
(a) Alternate straight and bias sides of the diamonds made from Template A as you match seam edges.

(b) Sew diamond #1 to diamond #2, beginning at the middle angle, and "setting in" 1/4". See *Accurate Piecing* (5), *Pinning Tails* (8D) and *Setting In* (9). Sew to the end of the seam. Open.

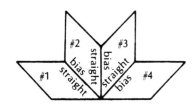

(c) Add diamond #3, "setting in" 1/4". Sew to end of seam. Finger press seam allowance of diamonds #1 and #2 to your left as you sew across it. Open.

(d) Add diamond #4, "setting in" 1/4". Sew to the end of the seam. Finger press seam allowance of diamonds #2 and #3 to your left as you sew across it.

(e) The third seam allowance will fall to the right naturally, so that all stitching lines of diamond #3 will be visible on the back of the block.

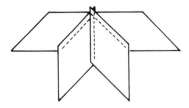

Bottom Half:
(a) Construct the bottom half of the star in the same manner as the top half, except reverse the starting order of the straight and bias sides.

3. Join the top and bottom halves of the star "setting in" 1/4" at the beginning and end of this center seam. See *Matching Horizontal Seam Joints* (8A, 8B and 8C).

4. "Set in" triangles made from Template C and squares made from Template B around the edges of the star until the block is completed, following the diagram showing the numbered order of the seams as you "set in" each patch. See *Setting In* (9). Sew all seams from the inside toward the outside edges of the block.

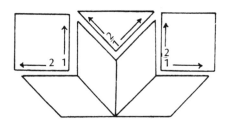

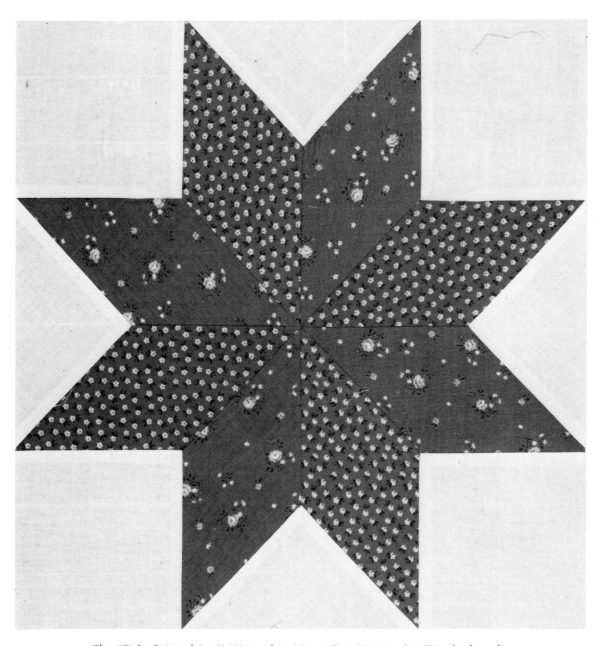

The "Eight-Pointed Star" ("Star of Le Moyne" or "Lemon Star") is the foundation of a wide range of more complex quilt patterns. This circle of eight diamonds is found in the center of the bed-size "Star of Bethlehem," "Lone Star," and "Sunburst" designs. When specific color rules are followed, or appliquéd centers or extra patches are added, the "Eight-Pointed Star" can become "Sunflowers," "Rising Sun," or several State Stars. Many tulip, lily, and peony patterns are derived from this basic diamond patchwork. Mastering the "Eight-Pointed Star" will give you the skill to attempt any of these countless variants.

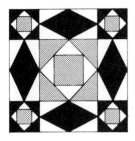

STORM AT SEA

The eight templates used to make this block appear on Plates 10 and 11.

1. Layer cut the following pieces. See *Layered Cutting* (3).

Template A . . . . .4 medium fabric
Template B . . . . .16 light fabric
Template C . . . . .16 dark fabric
Template D . . . . .4 dark fabric
Template E . . . . .16 light fabric
Template F . . . . .1 medium fabric
Template G . . . . .4 light fabric
Template H . . . . .4 medium fabric

2. This pattern is made by constructing three basic units and then combining them to make the finished block.

Unit One:

(a) Sew a triangle made from Template B to a square made from Template A. Open.

(b) Continue sewing triangles made from Template B to the square made from Template A, following the numbered order of the diagram. Clip tails.

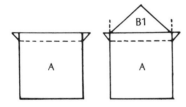

(c) Add four triangles made from Template C to this unit in the same manner. Keep the unit wrong side up as you sew. See *Stitching Through the Λ's* (8B).
(d) Repeat the above instructions, making three additional units.

Unit Two:

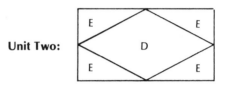

(a) Sew four triangles made from Template E to the diamond made from Template D.
(b) Make three additional units.

Unit Three:

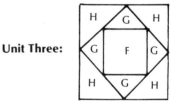

(a) Following the diagrams and directions for Unit One, sew four triangles made from Template G to the square made from Template F.
(b) Sew four triangles made from Template H to this unit in the same manner.
3. Following the block diagram arrange the completed units.
4. Join the vertical seams. See *Chain Sewing the Entire Block with Visible Chain* (7A).
5. Sew the horizontal seams. See *Matching Horizontal Seam Joints* (8A, 8B and 8C).

"Storm at Sea" (also called "Rolling Stone") combines straight edged squares, triangles, and diamonds to create the circular optical illusion of swirling, tumbling movement. The success of the optical illusion is dependent on the quilt maker's effective division of light, medium, and dark shades of colors among the geometric forms of the pattern.

GRANDMOTHER'S FLOWER GARDEN

The template used to make this quilt appears on plate 12.

1. Layer cut the following pieces. See *Layered Cutting* (3).

Template A . . . . .1 bright fabric
Template A . . . . .6 light fabric
Template A . . . . .12 dark fabric

2. Cut one 14 1/2'' square of fabric for backing.

NOTE: The beginning and end of every seam in this block uses the "setting in" technique. See Setting In (9).

---

3. Seam a light hexagon to the center hexagon, starting and stopping 1/4'' from the raw edges.

4. Add five more light hexagons around the center hexagon, "setting in" all seams.
5. Connect all the vertical seams of the inner ring, making sure that the seam allowances at the corners

are free.
6. Following the above instructions, add the hexagons of the outer ring. *NOTE: Every other hexagon in the outer ring has two connecting seams to the inner ring.*
7. Connect all of the vertical seams of the inner ring, following the "setting in" technique.
8. Press the back of the block so that all vertical seams fan in a clockwise direction.

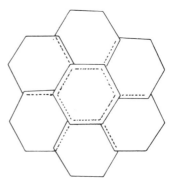

9. Press under the 1/4'' seam allowance of the outside edges of the flower. See *Pressing Technique for Angled Edges* (12A).
10. Appliqué the flower to the backing. See *Invisible Appliqué Stitch* (12C).

The "Grandmother's Flower Garden" pattern ("Martha Washington's Flower Garden," "Grandma's Dreams") is a descendant of the European mosaic or honeycomb designs, which used a single patch, the hexagon. Mosaic designs grow, hexagon by hexagon, until the overall pattern is completed.

"Grandmother's Flower Garden" simplifies the assembly of the quilt top by organizing the hexagons into two rings around a central hexagon. Thus, the flowers of the garden are created. Another row of hexagons, the garden path, is added to connect the flower beds.

Making one "Grandmother's Flower" block of 19 hexagons will help you decide whether to tackle a full-size "Grandmother's Flower Garden" quilt, which might have 1000 or more hexagons (of this size) to piece.

DRUNKARD'S PATH VARIATIONS

The two templates used to make all of the variations of "Drunkard's Path" appear on Plate 13.

The sample block and the instructions are for "Harvest Moon," one of the many variations of "Drunkard's Path". The same basic instructions apply to all other variations; the difference occurs in the number of colors and the placement of the squares in the block.

1. Layer cut the following pieces. See *Layered Cutting* (3) and *Curves* (3B).

        Template A . . . . .16 dark fabric
        Template B . . . . .16 light fabric

2. Clip the crescent square made from Template A along the curve.

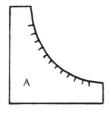

3. Pin a crescent square made from Template A to a wedge made from Template B with the clipped crescent square on the top. See *Sewing Curves* (10).

4. Sew, easing to fit, using a short, #15 stitch.

5. Arrange the assembled squares, following the block diagram.

6. Chain sew the entire block. See *Chain Sewing the Entire Block* (7) and *Butting Seams* (8A).

FOOLS PUZZLE   RIPPLING WATER

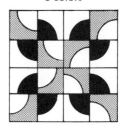

DRUNKARD'S PATH
3 colors

This graceful combination of curves and lines makes numerous abstract designs and visual images, using only two shapes. Some pattern names may overlap, but each one gives us a clear picture of a situation or object in our lives. Colorful names describe a tippler's faltering steps home or the grandeur of a "Trip Around the World". There are puzzles to confuse a fool, "Cleopatra," and even "Solomon". And there are scenes from nature—"Rippling Water," "Harvest Moon," "Falling Timbers".

"Drunkard's Path Variations" are traditionally shown in two colors, sometimes three. Be inventive. Try four.

DRESDEN PLATE

The four templates used to make this block appear on Plate 14.

1. Layer cut the following pieces. See *Layered Cutting* (3).

Template A ....16 assorted fabrics
Template B ....4 one color

2. Cut one 14 1/2″ square of fabric for backing.

3. Arrange the wedges following the block diagram.

4. Begin the seams of the wedges at the outside edge, "setting in" 1/4″. Seam all the way to the inside circle. See *Setting In* (9).

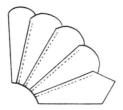

5. Continue joining the wedges until the "plate" is completed.

6. Press or baste under the 1/4″ seam allowance on the inside of the circle.

7. Using the Pressing Template C, press under the 1/4″ seam allowance on the outside curve of the wedges made from Template A. See *Pressing Curved Edges* (12B).

8. Press under the outside edges of the wedges made from Template B. See *Pressing Angled Edges* (12 A).

9. Center and pin the "plate" on the backing square.

10. Appliqué the "plate" to the backing using the invisible appliqué stitch. See *Invisible Appliqué Stitch* (12C). If you want the center of the plate to be a different color from the backing—as in the sample block—baste a circle, of the chosen fabric made from Template D onto the backing before the final appliqué of the "plate". The center circle must be appliquéd first to ensure smoothness of the finished "plate".

You can choose to make your "Dresden Plate" using all curved wedges, all pointed wedges, 4 curved wedges and 16 pointed wedges, alternating curved and pointed wedges, or, as shown in the photograph.

THREE-DIMENSIONAL DAHLIA

The five templates used to make this quilt block appear on plates 15 and 16.

1. Layer cut the following pieces. See *Layered Cutting* (3).

    Template A . . . . .8 print I
    Template B . . . . .4 light
    Template C . . . . .4 light
    Template D . . . . .8 print II

2. Cut one of the following:

    Template E . . . . .1 print III

3. Clip along the curves of the wedge made from Template A.

4. Seam the four triangles made from Template B to the right straight side of four wedges made from Template A, making certain the long side of the triangle is on the left, as shown. Open.

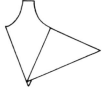

5. Seam the four squares made from Template C to the right, straight side of the other four wedges made from Template A. Open.

6. Sew a "petal" made from Template D to the left curve of each wedge-triangle unit and each wedge-

square unit as shown. Follow the directional arrow of the diagram, and stretch the wedge curve to fit the petal curve. The petal will be on the bottom as you sew. See *Sewing Curves* (10).

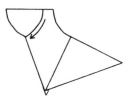

7. Following the block diagram, sew a petal-wedge-triangle unit to a petal-wedge-square unit to a petal-wedge-triangle unit and so forth until the outside edges of the block are joined. Sew each seam from the outside edge of the block toward the inside curved edge with a petal on the bottom, stretching the wedge curve to fit the petal curve. "Butt seams" at the point of the petal so that the petal seam allowance is pinned away from the petal. See *Butting Seams* (8A).

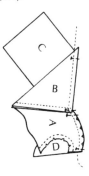

8. Press the petal seams towards the wedge.

9. Gather the circle opening of this unit to fit the circle made from Template E. Use a long basting stitch and a 1/4'' seam. Arrange the gathers in the petals only, so that the narrow ends of the wedges are perfectly flat.

10. Mark the circle made from Template E in eight equal sections.

11. Match and pin the narrow ends of the wedges to the circle marks. Pin the center of each gathered petal to ensure security and the flatness of the circle.

12. Sew with a 1/4'' seam.

"Three-Dimensional Dahlia," also known as "Red Dahlia," "Gathered Dahlia," and "Star Flower," has been a popular pattern in the Pennsylvania Dutch Country for many years. You have worked hard to achieve attractive, evenly gathered petals for this block. Be sure the fabric you choose emphasizes this focal point.

METRIC CONVERSION TABLE

CONVERTING INCHES TO CENTIMETERS AND YARDS TO METERS

mm — millimeters   cm — centimeters   m — meters

INCHES INTO MILLIMETERS AND CENTIMETERS
(Slightly rounded off for convenience)

inches	mm		cm	inches	cm	inches	cm	inches	cm
1/8	3mm			5	12.5	21	53.5	38	96.5
1/4	6mm			5½	14	22	56	39	99
3/8	10mm	or	1cm	6	15	23	58.5	40	101.5
1/2	13mm	or	1.3cm	7	18	24	61	41	104
5/8	15mm	or	1.5cm	8	20.5	25	63.5	42	106.5
3/4	20mm	or	2cm	9	23	26	66	43	109
7/8	22mm	or	2.2cm	10	25.5	27	68.5	44	112
1	25mm	or	2.5cm	11	28	28	71	45	114.5
1¼	32mm	or	3.2cm	12	30.5	29	73.5	46	117
1½	38mm	or	3.8cm	13	33	30	76	47	119.5
1¾	45mm	or	4.5cm	14	35.5	31	79	48	122
2	50mm	or	5cm	15	38	32	81.5	49	124.5
2½	65mm	or	6.5cm	16	40.5	33	84	50	127
3	75mm	or	7.5cm	17	43	34	86.5		
3½	90mm	or	9cm	18	46	35	89		
4	100mm	or	10cm	19	48.5	36	91.5		
4½	115mm	or	11.5cm	20	51	37	94		

YARDS TO METERS
(Slightly rounded off for convenience)

yards	meters	yards	meters	yards	meters	yards	meters	yards	meters
1/8	0.15	2⅛	1.95	4⅛	3.80	6⅛	5.60	8⅛	7.45
1/4	0.25	2¼	2.10	4¼	3.90	6¼	5.75	8¼	7.55
3/8	0.35	2⅜	2.20	4⅜	4.00	6⅜	5.85	8⅜	7.70
1/2	0.50	2½	2.30	4½	4.15	6½	5.95	8½	7.80
5/8	0.60	2⅝	2.40	4⅝	4.25	6⅝	6.10	8⅝	7.90
3/4	0.70	2¾	2.55	4¾	4.35	6¾	6.20	8¾	8.00
7/8	0.80	2⅞	2.65	4⅞	4.50	6⅞	6.30	8⅞	8.15
1	0.95	3	2.75	5	4.60	7	6.40	9	8.25
1⅛	1.05	3⅛	2.90	5⅛	4.70	7⅛	6.55	9⅛	8.35
1¼	1.15	3¼	3.00	5¼	4.80	7¼	6.65	9¼	8.50
1⅜	1.30	3⅜	3.10	5⅜	4.95	7⅜	6.75	9⅜	8.60
1½	1.40	3½	3.20	5½	5.05	7½	6.90	9½	8.70
1⅝	1.50	3⅝	3.35	5⅝	5.15	7⅝	7.00	9⅝	8.80
1¾	1.60	3¾	3.45	5¾	5.30	7¾	7.10	9¾	8.95
1⅞	1.75	3⅞	3.55	5⅞	5.40	7⅞	7.20	9⅞	9.05
2	1.85	4	3.70	6	5.50	8	7.35	10	9.15

AVAILABLE FABRIC WIDTHS

25"	65cm	50"	127cm
27"	70cm	54"/56"	140cm
35"/36"	90cm	58"/60"	150cm
39"	100cm	68"/70"	175cm
44"/45"	115cm	72"	180cm
48"	122cm		

AVAILABLE ZIPPER LENGTHS

4"	10cm	10"	25cm	22"	55cm
5"	12cm	12"	30cm	24"	60cm
6"	15cm	14"	35cm	26"	65cm
7"	18cm	16"	40cm	28"	70cm
8"	20cm	18"	45cm	30"	75cm
9"	22cm	20"	50cm		

THE TEMPLATES

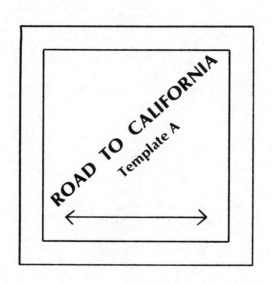

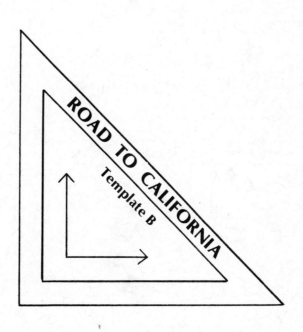

PLATE 1

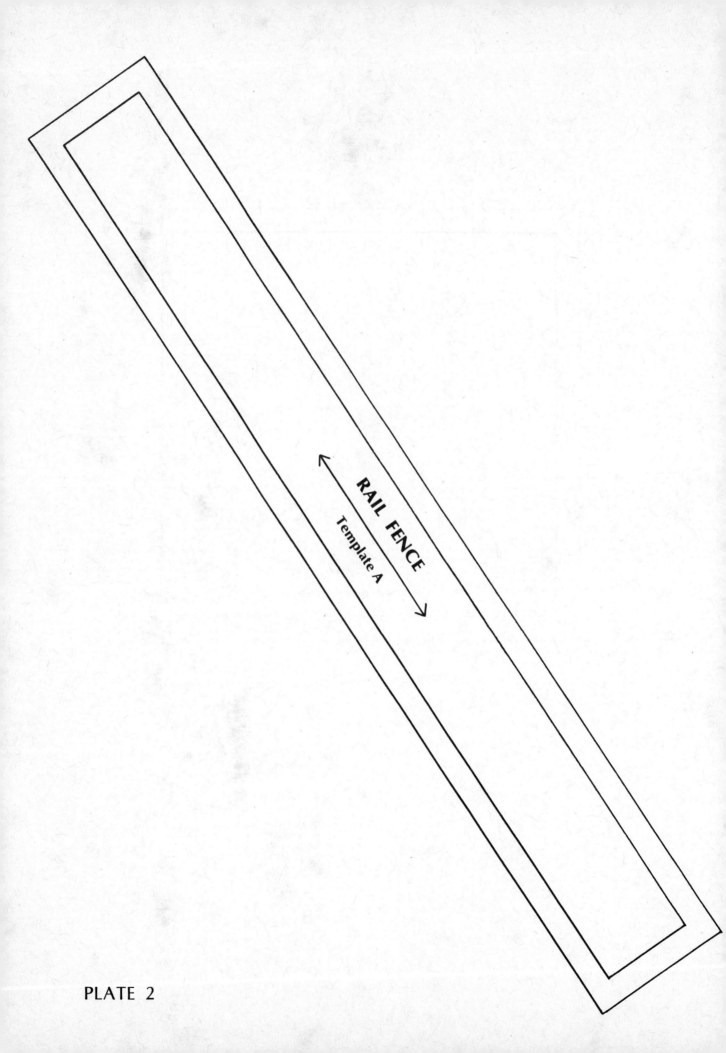

RAIL FENCE

Template A

PLATE 2

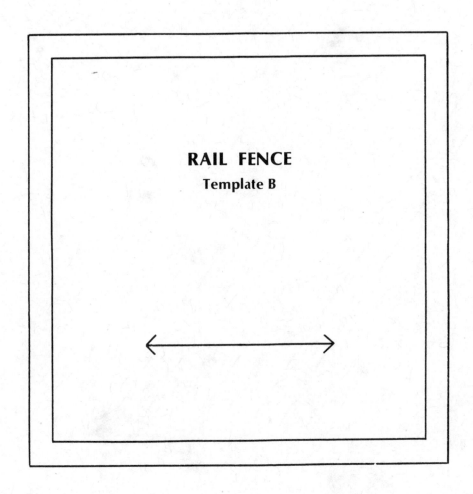

RAIL FENCE
Template B

PLATE 3

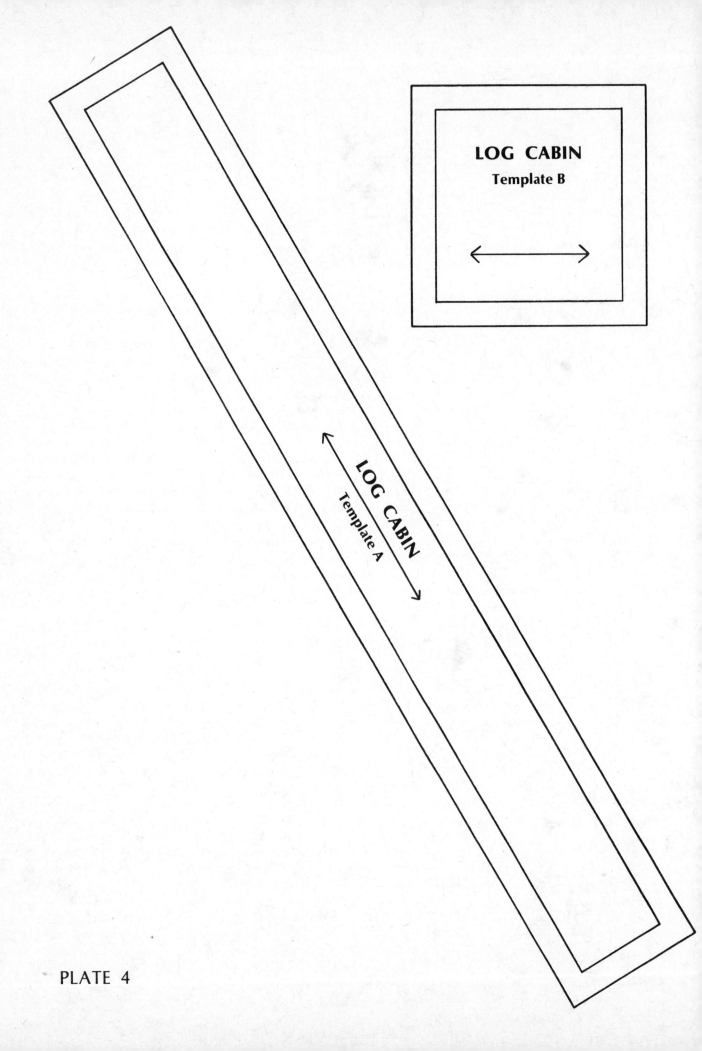

LOG CABIN

Template B

LOG CABIN

Template A

PLATE 4

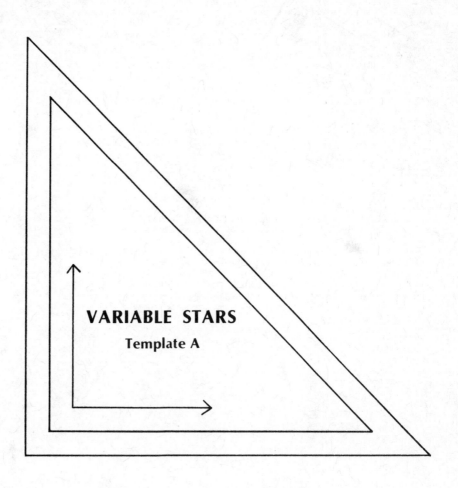

VARIABLE STARS

Template A

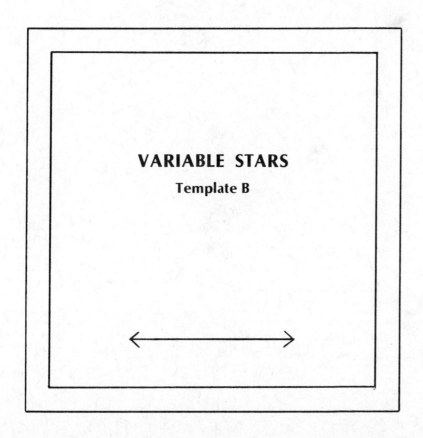

VARIABLE STARS

Template B

PLATE 5

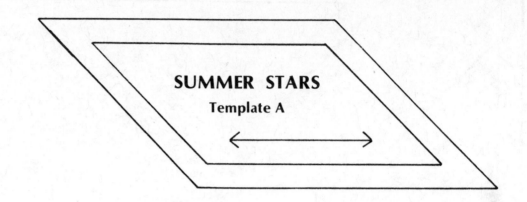

SUMMER STARS
Template A

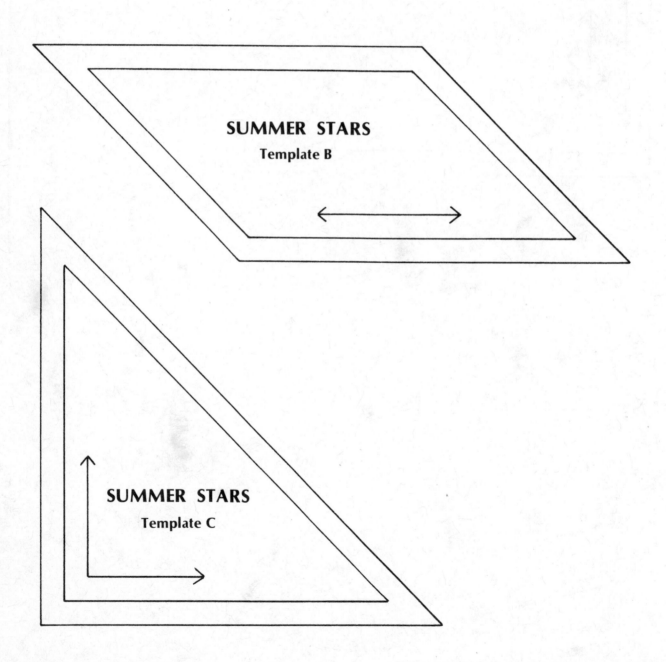

SUMMER STARS
Template B

SUMMER STARS
Template C

PLATE 6

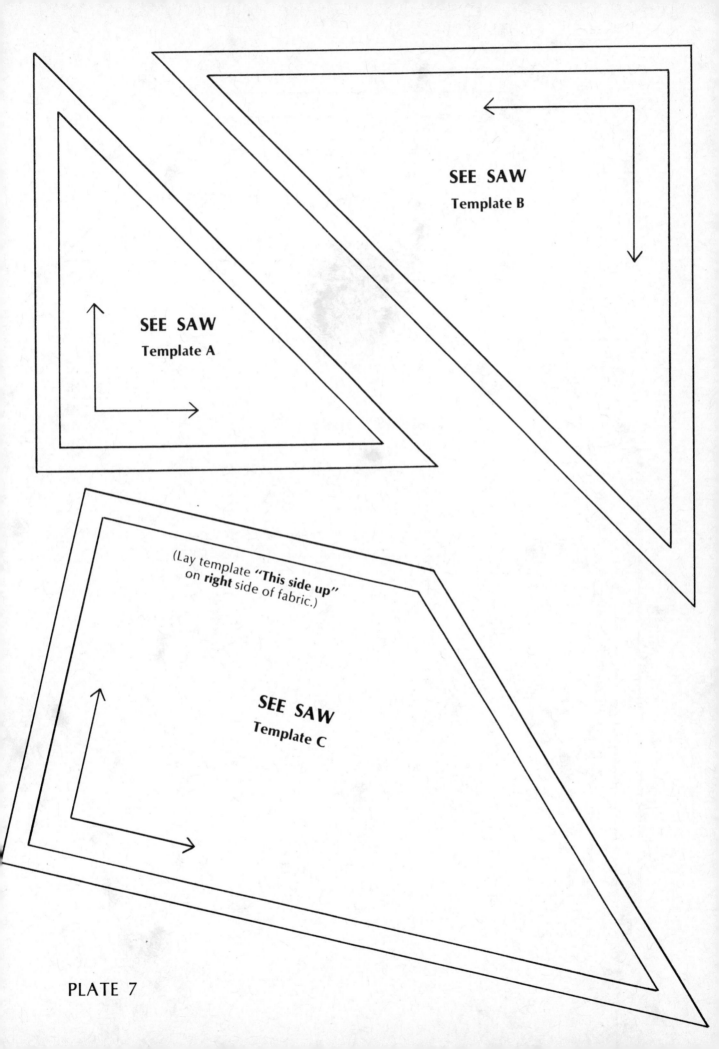

SEE SAW
Template B

SEE SAW
Template A

(Lay template "This side up" on right side of fabric.)

SEE SAW
Template C

PLATE 7

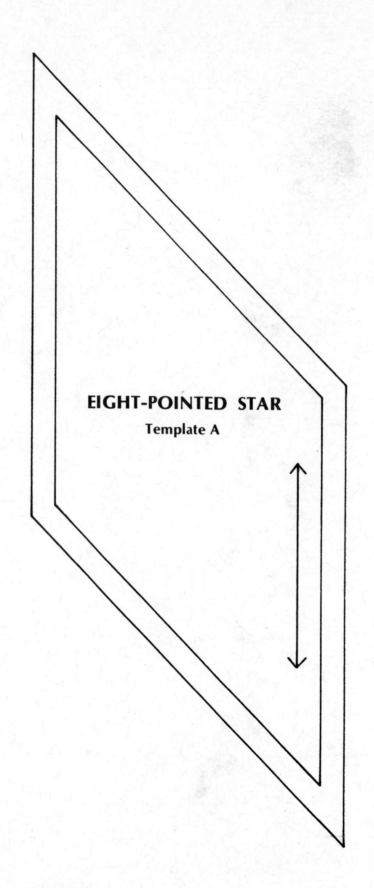

EIGHT-POINTED STAR

Template A

PLATE 8

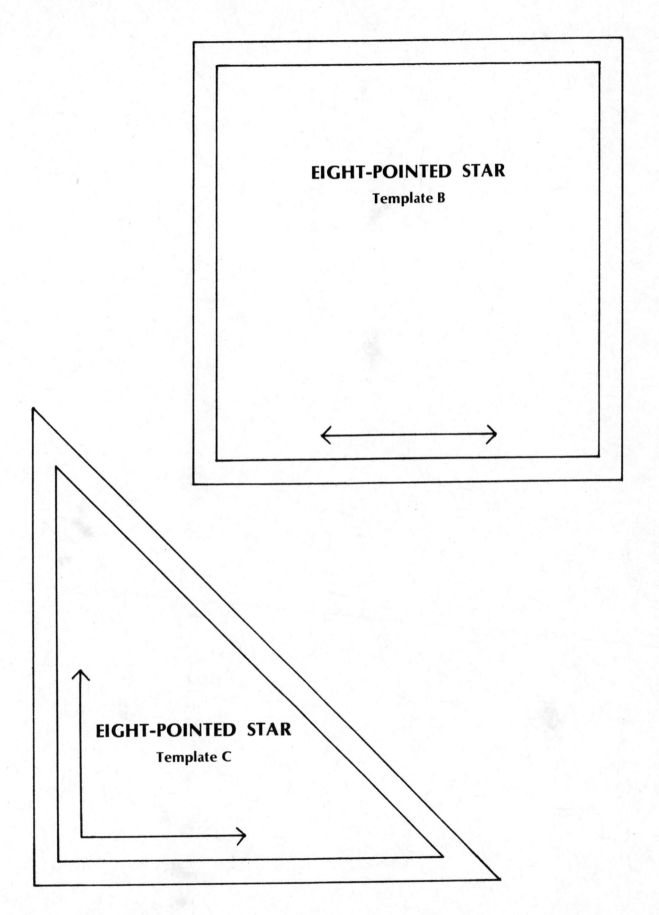

EIGHT-POINTED STAR
Template B

EIGHT-POINTED STAR
Template C

PLATE 9

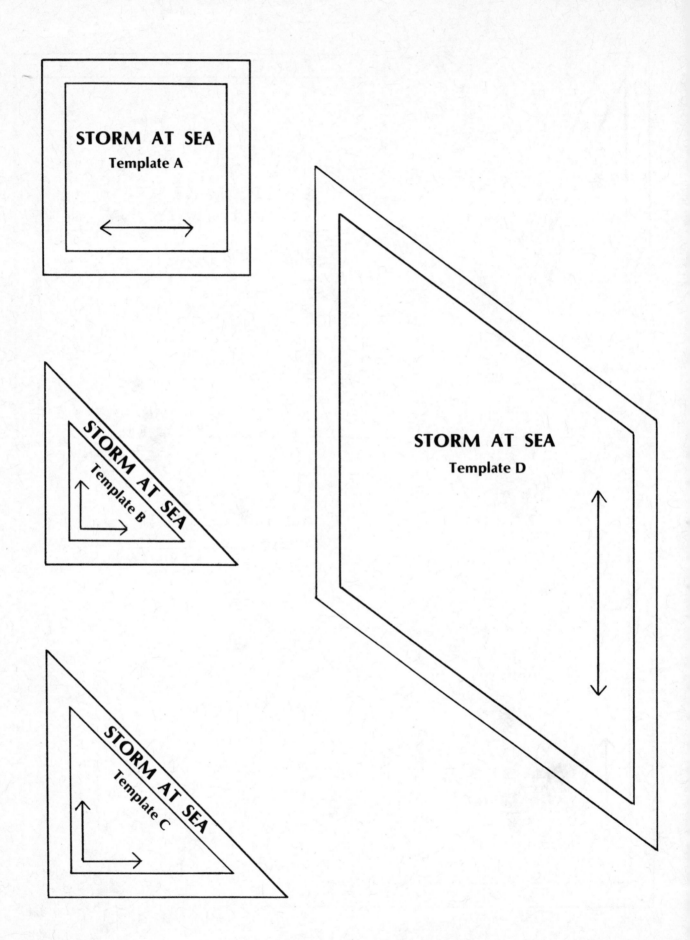

STORM AT SEA
Template A

STORM AT SEA
Template B

STORM AT SEA
Template C

STORM AT SEA
Template D

PLATE 10

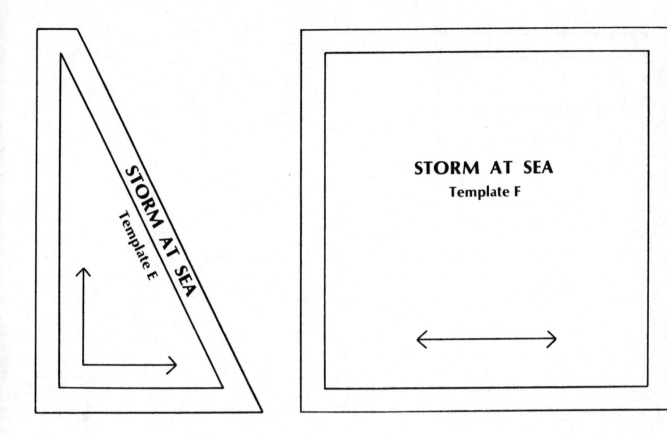

STORM AT SEA
Template E

STORM AT SEA
Template F

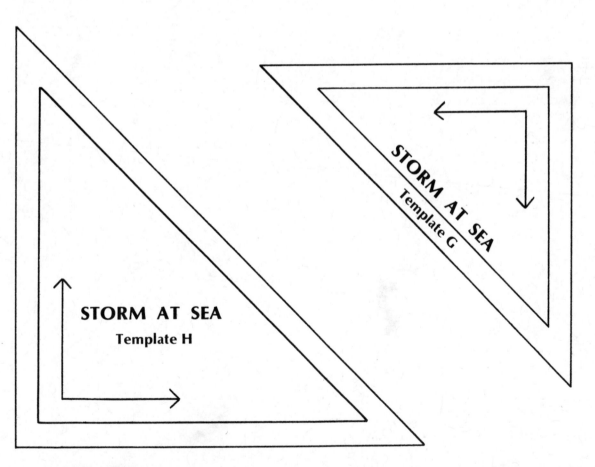

STORM AT SEA
Template G

STORM AT SEA
Template H

PLATE 11

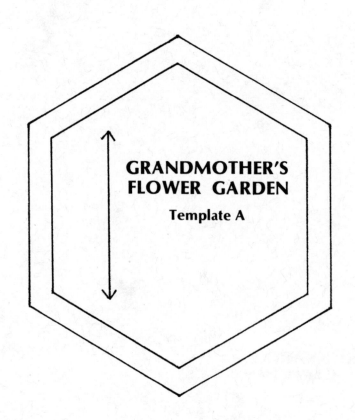

**GRANDMOTHER'S
FLOWER GARDEN**

Template A

PLATE 12

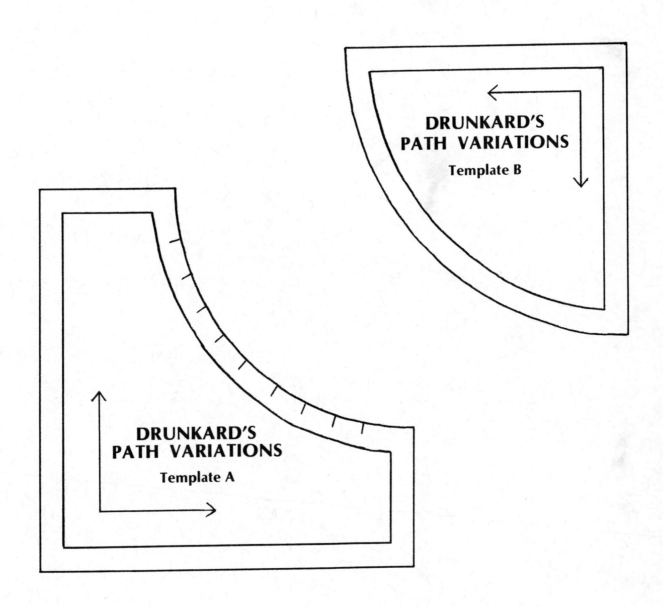

DRUNKARD'S PATH VARIATIONS

Template B

DRUNKARD'S PATH VARIATIONS

Template A

PLATE 13

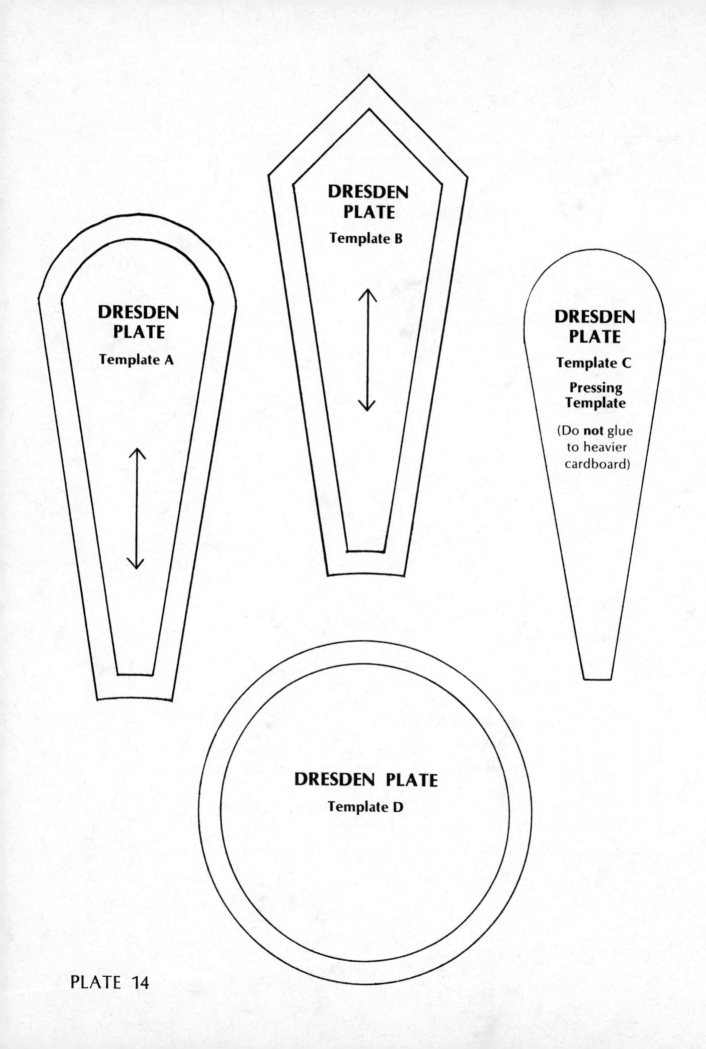

DRESDEN PLATE

Template A

DRESDEN PLATE

Template B

DRESDEN PLATE

Template C

Pressing Template

(Do **not** glue to heavier cardboard)

DRESDEN PLATE

Template D

PLATE 14

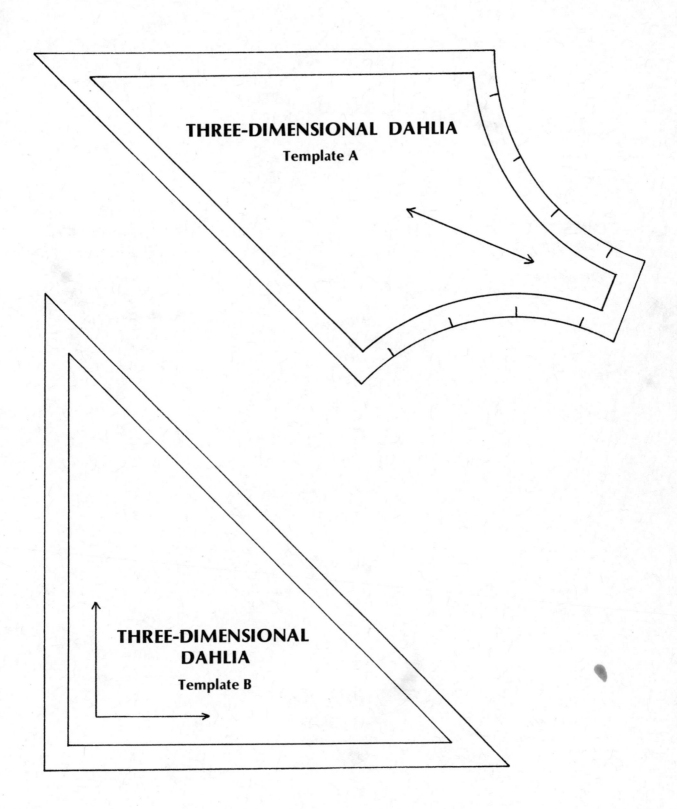

THREE-DIMENSIONAL DAHLIA

Template A

THREE-DIMENSIONAL DAHLIA

Template B

PLATE 15

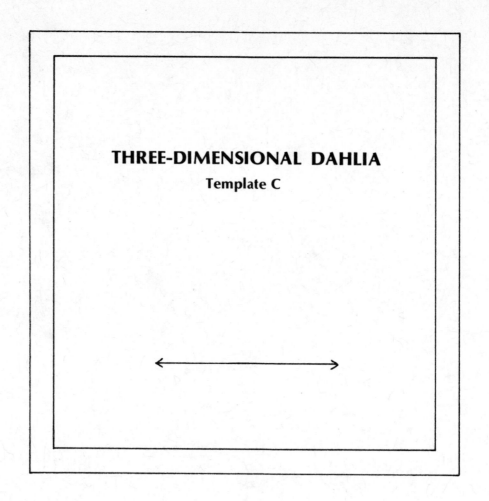

THREE-DIMENSIONAL DAHLIA

Template C

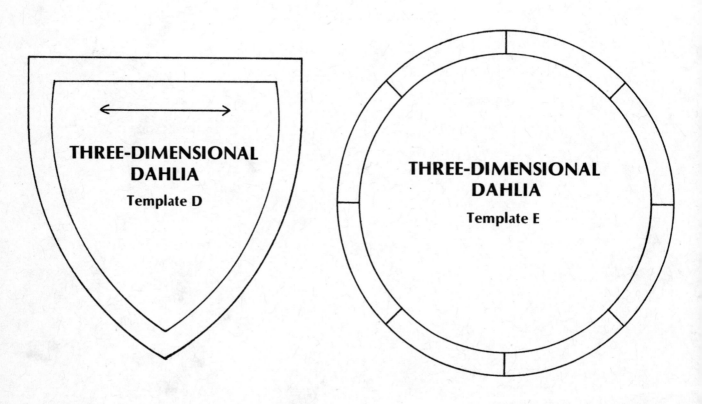

THREE-DIMENSIONAL DAHLIA

Template D

THREE-DIMENSIONAL DAHLIA

Template E

PLATE 16